D0809024

A STORY INTERRUPTED

OTHER TITLES FROM AIRLIE PRESS

A Story

Interrupted

POEMS

Connie Soper

Airlie Press
PORTLAND OREGON

2022

Airlie Press is supported by book sales, by contributions to the press from its supporters, and by the work donated by all the poet-editors of the press.

P.O. Box 13325
Portland OR 97213
www.airliepress.org
email: airliepress@gmail.com

First Edition
    ISBN 978-1-950404-10-0
    Library of Congress record available at https://lccn.loc.gov/2021952091

Printed in the United States of America
    Cover and book design by N. Putens
    Author photo by: Trav Williams, Broken Banjo Photography
    Cover artwork: "Striving for Resolution" Painting by Christopher Mathie
    www.christophermathie.com

for Cris
and
for Marguerite

CONTENTS

Three LAST POUR

A STORY INTERRUPTED

ONE   *Mapping Boundaries*

ANTHEM

Joshua Tree National Park

Bend to one knee
or stand with hand over heart.
Sing an anthem or don't
voice one at all.

          Just claim this desert as your own,
with its hard white light
and punishing heat. Claim the boulders tumbled
            into a wonderland
baked to umber and ochre
until the sun dissolves into the washes and fissures
and nothing is the same but nothing has changed.

Name the Joshuas for that seeker of the promised land
who raised his hands in prayer.

Praise your own god
or worship the dogma of the sun. Tell me
           how you cherish this creation
as it is meant to be: unviolated and whole.

Allow yourself to tremble within the holy
soul of the Mojave
           gobsmacked humbled unbruised.

AMANDA'S TRAIL

In 1864, Amanda De-Cuys, a blind Coos woman, was removed from her home
and forced to walk some 50 miles to be relocated at the Coast Reservation near
what is now Yachats, Oregon.

It was her way to embrace circles of seasons
in an abundance of bulbs, roots, berries;
to harvest mussels in the low and salty estuary—
until she became a refugee in her own homeland.

It was her way to lay the dead
in canoes hung from branches, always
facing west. Those boats would sway
in the breeze as souls rowed into the next world.
Which of us wouldn't enter eternity like that?

It was her way to leave gifts
for that long journey: basket, knife, blanket—
until those gifts were stolen for souvenirs.
It was her way to trust the shaman,
until the diseases came and there were no more
living to tend to the dying.

Today, we lace our boots and ready packs
to step into forest's ripe and sudden smells
on the flanks of Cape Perpetua.
The same cliffs, chasms, streams, rocks.
The same churning waves in the distance.

The path before us curves like the parenthesis of history.
We can't see its end as we cross over a bridge,
traverse switchbacks, follow twisting trail
to pause at a knoll overlooking the expansive sea.
Cedars press green spirit-weave against the sky—
dappled with light, rooted in darkness.

AMERICAN LOGGERS, 1939

after Dorothea Lange

The deep green river chokes
on backwoods bounty, churning
its industry downstream to the mill.
In the creamy fading light of day: silence.

No more rhythmic thump of axes, their report
startling birds from branches. Quiet enough
to smell pitch bleeding from pines
and the sweet perfume of felled wood.

Five men rest calloused palms on long-
necked tools, rooted to stillness.
The youngest poses hand on hip, eyes
on tomorrow's prey: treetops grazing the sky.

He sets a rigging, straps the harness, cinches
buckles to shimmy feet-first up the scaled hide
he will climb, higher than the owl's nest,
to amputate mossy limbs one by one—

with forest's enormity at his feet, count
its rings: 200, 250, until he loses track.

IN THE COMMONWEALTH

Montpelier, Virginia

Perfect green hillocks rise between hedgerows,
amid stands of black walnut.
Cedars of Lebanon, seeded in France,
still thrive on the mansion grounds;
fence slats define a pastoral tableau.
Horses—descendants, perhaps, from DuPont's stables,
fatten in the field as they consider tourists
with bucolic indifference.
We cross the mowed path to the portico
strong with Roman columns.
In the dining room, cardboard cutouts
form an animated theater around the table:
Jefferson, Franklin, Jackson, Dolley with her teacup.
Madison's manservant stands in the corner,
holding a tray—Paul Jennings, sold for $200 in 1846.
Imagine the conversations, the docent says,
a polite discourse of gentle persuasion.

Up the carpeted stairs, pink-flocked walls
adorned with ornamental sconces—
to the library replete with books by learned men.
Supple leather spines suffused with warm shades
of butter, bourbon, cherry. In this very room,

Madison conjured a republic born of ideals,
plucked from measured words
of poets and philosophers. Here, he overlooked
Blue Ridge vistas, fertile soil and great expanse
of his plantation. All that he owned.

ARCHAEOLOGY

Corbridge Roman Museum

Cropped paths maze the curated grounds past
reconstructed stone walls, aqueduct

and ancient granary to River Tyne, where
the Romans bathed. Picture placards reimagine

the city, its tranquil industry after the conquest.
Timelines on the museum wall catalog

inventions of war:
spear, sword, catapult, pistol.

Weapons arranged under glass cases
like fine works of art. Caltrops, hand-forged

to hobble enemy cavalry, resemble huge jacks,
a children's game. Arrowheads unearthed from

the dig and still lashed to their spears, crafted
chamfron to protect a horse's head—copper filament

twisted into shapes of dolphins and eagles.
How beautiful and bronzed they must have looked—

men and horses decorated in battle costumes
adorned with belts, straps and slides,

ornamental buttons and hip fasteners. All those shiny
objects glittering in the sun as they rode away.

BOY, FOURTEEN, 1936

after Dorothea Lange

Old oak and cottonwood trees straddle
the American River, a brown season's leaves
drifting on its sour water. Crops are done;
fruit rots on frozen vines, pecked at by birds.

Small boy in cotton overalls stands alone outside
a tar paper shack under canvas overhang—
rocking chair stilled on the worn fabric of grass
next to rusted hubcaps, pile of plywood.

On the other side of Dorothea's camera: older boy.
Half-child, half-man, his beauty sears
the ragged earth, overwhelming stippled shadows.
Half-rooted, half-soaring, he knows what he sees:

autumnal flight of geese guided by instinct to some
better place, formation unfurling an alphabet he has yet
to learn. Vowels open and round, winged "V"
a moving silhouette against the orange harvest moon.

COMMON GROUND

The crew arrives
on a flatbed truck
rumbling in second gear
over a rutted county road;
                    chorus of

hardhats and orange safety
vests as workers chart the path
between little fluorescent flags,
mapping boundaries

                    where a fern-fringed trail
will wind among Sitka spruce,
skirt the ravine, switchback
hillsides purpled with foxglove,
across the shallow brook.

Brush cleared, bramble hacked,
slopes shored; they dig
holes for planting signposts:
                    welcome, hikers
don't pick the flowers
don't feed the wildlife, no
trespassing beyond the fence.

At day's end,
chatter of satisfaction
from good and solid work,
steering the truck into
a night of dreamless sleep.

Tiny stars pinprick the sky,
barely visible behind scrim
of coastal fog.

Forest creatures chirp and click
their nocturnal languages,
scurry hollow to burrow,
                        nest to snag,

through branches, scrub, twisted roots;
under and over
the yellow construction tape.

PEA PICKER, 1939

after Dorothea Lange

He stirs from dreams
of snow; never stood at a window

to watch it pillow quilted mounds
over a world thickened and slowed

under the white weight of winter,
each flake its own creation.

He knows blizzards of grit, places
where dust curtains the horizon with no

certainty of ending. Even gravity is confused
as stars shiver in the wide apron of night sky.

Here, in a California valley rich with heat
and harvest, the pea picker bends

with practiced choreography, dips, rises, hoists
a brimming basket to his shoulder

balanced by fingertips. He crisscrosses
symmetrical rows, measured steps along planks

over the irrigation ditch to the weighmaster:
22 cents a hamper. Sure-footed and nimble,

like a skater gliding across a frozen lake.

TREE

Starved of light or water—
fungus-rot eating it like a cancer
from the inside out—even the giant
sequoia will topple one day. This shore pine

done in by the fury
of winter as I listened to wind that gusted
heaving waves over the Pacific.
All night that sea-power
shuddered and thumped. The tree
did not surrender

one branch at a time; an entire body
collapsed—trunk and limbs
clinging to roots that connected it
to earth. Now it waits for chainsaw
and cremation. The ground beneath the
fallen piney crown is soft and sodden;
the air still, silent. Yesterday a house

of branches grew outside my window.
Now, the hollow where life uprooted itself
yawns like a mouth without a voice.
There's a hole in the landscape, phantom
emptiness against the sky.

NEITHER/NOR

March, 2020

Spindly branches claw
the sky like bony bird feet.
Neither upside down
nor right side up.

No memories of this
curious season.
Nothing to remember.
Late winter, early spring:
what's the difference
with streets this dark,
the city not yet awake?
Neither day nor night,

dim light halos
kitchen's earthenware jars,
kettle steaming.
The room is silent
but for unfamiliar voices on the radio:
neither hope nor despair.
   social/distant
   community/island
   connect/alone

The old maples soldier
in place the way
they always have, readying
their fulsome deciduous
coats. Neither barren

nor blossoming,
they press their shapes above
architecture of roofs
and all the lives sleeping below
those eaves and rafters.

TERMINUS

So many old European cities promised cathedrals
and castles, staid and stately rooms where treaties
were signed—always an ornate architecture, rich

with patina-copper domes, steeples and turrets.
When my feet tired of museums bragging
ancient relics, and when a polluted hot noise pressed down

over the somber monuments, I boarded a bus,
any bus—paid a few pesos, drachmas, centimes—
and rode to the end of the line. Not for the journey

itself, or its destination, but for the sake of not knowing
where it would take me as that bus lurched
into unmapped margins of a city. Grand avenues

blooming geraniums gave way to glimpses
of villages within the metropolis, lively with cafes,
blue-uniformed children. Every neighborhood's pride

its plaza—boys circled footballs in the ragged
handkerchief of a field as pigeons shook
themselves from the belfry at sonorous

sounds of bells ringing the evening mass. One by one
passengers disembarked until the bus arrived
at the end of its route. *Terminus*, the driver called out.

Same word, I learned, in so many languages.

READING ANOTHER LIFE

April rain, ginger tea, yellow tulips
in a blue bowl as I read
another life. Today, a ranger's story
in the High Sierras, how he disappeared
somewhere
among chasms, boulders, streams.
Swallowed into wilderness.

His solitude not a lonely place—
silhouette of sequoias backlit
against a compass of stars, topography
etched by grandeur of granite. Meadow
to ridgeline, guided by certainty of purpose.
Still, he lost his way, the mystery not *why*
but *how* he found his worth alone, deep
in Kings Canyon. How it found him.

Not a life for me, with its frigid dawns,
precarious footing. I'm grateful, though,
for views afforded beyond this room defined
by corner, walls, ceiling.

His happiness was born from listening
to crack of glaciers melting,
musicality of streams as they washed
over riverstone. I hear rain, the sound
of pages turning.

DEAR SMOKE, DEAR FIRE

It's your season of char. Again,
hot ash confettis the foothills
above Klamath Lake, while in

New Mexico birds plummet mid-flight.
Their soft bodies litter arroyos, flung
along banks of dry riverbeds.

The ornithologists spread little
carcasses into a quilt of feathers, wing
to grounded wing. Now, violet-

green swallows and yellow warblers
are sealed in Ziploc bags,
specimens for the necropsies.

Tiny scalpels cut into them.
Tweezers pry open lungs, heart—
for proof you confused them

in migration. So many ways
you sicken this blue planet: forests singed,
pestilent air, weave of nest unraveled.

Yet, you want more. Here, take this
turquoise feather—
even flightless, see how it shimmers.

Just don't take the whole wing.
Do not siphon their song from our memory.
Let us keep this much.

JOLABOKAFLOD

*Icelanders give each other books on Christmas Eve and then spend the night
reading. This tradition began during World War II, when many other com-
modities were restricted, and is called Jolabokaflod, or "Christmas book flood."*

During the war, butter
was rationed, sugar doled out
by the spoonful. No Christmas candy
tucked into children's shoes. But

paper—plentiful enough; pages
cut for books bound with heft
and spine—an abundance
during want.

In this country—so cold its name
is ice— an alphabet rolls
rich with vowels and dangling umlauts.
Language rooted in Poetic Edda, saga
and myth. All the many names for *snowflakes*.

On solstice nights the goddess
of the north wind rimes windows
with her white coat. Stars dazzle
and shiver like an inverted
snow globe. Cedar logs ablaze, lamps
lit in all the houses for readers
to row those little paper boats
into the swell of the flood.

CHILD, LOST

She's a stranger in a small girl's face—
brown-eyed beam of peripheral light
pulsing pixels from the television.
Someone else voices her story in a language
she does not speak.

I press the remote to see her world
in stopped motion—
the whole muted landscape:
>   mattress, cement floor, windowless room.

She is not my daughter.
I am no child's mother; but don't tell me
the childless cannot grieve a world
where a mother orphans her baby to save it.
Where hope is a barren road leaving Guatemala,
embrace of *familia* not enough.

I, too, would cross the rivered divide between us,
brush her hair until it sparks stars,
lay her into the pillowed embrace of dreamless sleep
so she can forget. No,

like a mother I would help her remember,
so she can rise to tell it all:
>   smell of disinfectant, stench of fear;
>   shapeless shadows on pocked walls;
>   metallic clang of doors closing;
>   the many ways to say *alone*.

VIRTUAL NOSTALGIA

Go ahead. Fly from a chair.
Navigate your laptop over the Blue Lagoon,
above massive ancient glaciers
to the sharp bite of a waterfall. Watch
from your living room as the Aurora Borealis
greens arctic skies; drone-cameras
zoom over thatched-roof farmhouses
to spy on the sheep, goats, and wild caribou. Down,

down, hovering above cities, streets, houses
where people like you eat breakfast
of smoked herring, yogurt, and coffee.

You long for it, like a melancholic music
rousing the ghosts
of your ancestors. Oh, sure, icecaps are melting
there, too; winters long and bleak; the cost
of beer and bread; a word
for watching weather through windows:
Gluggavedur. Say it.

Download yourself to stand at the coordinates
of brisk and briny. Where citizens wear eyes
the color of a robin's egg. Whales breaching. Volcanos
smoldering over their rims.
You, descending into Reykjavik, return to a place
you've never been. Like a hand you've always held,
a face you've always known.

FALLING

In the season between trillium and foxglove,
we hike the high trail above Short Sand Creek.
The path is slick with clay and wet leaves, rich
with loamy smells of not-quite-summer.
Far below, the stream ends its cathartic journey.
I am an animal,

but not the surefooted kind.
No yak balanced on Himalayan cliffs. These unhooved
feet betray, no longer connecting me to this or any earth—

down the slope in all its shades of newborn green,
my body comes to rest in a cradle of moss and twigs,
among the decaying trunks of fallen
trees. Below me only air,
horizontal emptiness. I cling to roots, ferns and branches—
ropes like a ladder to the light—
and hoist myself back onto the spinning world.

The stream still ribbons its liquid over rocks as
we walk the path back to the road that brought us here,
and will bring us here again.

LETTER TO THE DISAPPEARED

                Dear Delphina, Dear Tamara, Dear Nicole,
Did you know you would ghost yourselves
from a dismal broken place when you vanished
along the Yellowhead Highway? Maybe
you tried to find your worth somewhere
along that road, a lonely lovely artery feeding
the heart of Canada.
                Both can be true at once.

                Dear Tina, Dear Amber, Dear Ramona,
Every translucent cell of your bodies erased—
hair, bone, fingernail—as if

you were scrubbed from this earth.
26, 69, 500…no one counted how many
First Nation women like you

were weighted with stones, wrapped in plastic
and dumped along the shallow
banks of the red
                Red River near the Winnipeg docks.

                Dear Angeline, Dear Dawn, Dear Lisa,
No witnesses when you went missing from a motel,
or a bus stop on an ordinary rainy street in Vancouver.

No one looked for you because maybe
you were high, selling sex
or having it forced from you. Both
                can be true at once.

So you vanished again in metal graveyard
of filing cabinets; death-sleep in manila folders
labeled with a case number. Now
               you are dots on a map.

               Dear Disappeared,
Those who remember march in your name,
drag the river, sift through ravines and ditches

deep in the backwoods to find you.
You are gone, and still they search.
               Everything can be true at once.

TWO *Spray of Salt*

SONNET FOR NEAHKAHNIE MOUNTAIN

The Tillamook people referred to Neahkahnie Mountain as "Place of the Creator"

This is where the continent ends. Land falls
away, limned in burnt ochre and steeping
copper-streaks aged by rain, wind, filaments
of light. Coastal fog veils the shore—ancestral
visitation. Tillamook people chose this home,
or it chose them, to carry their spirit-lore
deep into the ferny forest, paths cut by elk.
Stories rowed and sung into salty estuaries,

mussels pried from these rough rocks. Fish so plenti-
ful they leapt from the sea. Shadows still rib the
mountain dark and rusty, wind knocking waves
from their deep source. Place of the creator: tides,
circling smoke, a mossy place we enter like
a new season—all slick, bountiful, wild.

NESTUCCA SPIT

September's gone—drifting into
a season measured by what's lost
or missing: light, leaves, summer's

long dreams. Blackberries shrivel
on unruly vines, late for picking.
We, too, are dying a little more—

no cure but to hike the long strand
of beach straddling ocean and bay.
The spit, brushed in its own barren

beauty: hillocks, dunes, seagrass
swaying brown upon brown. Shore pines
lean into their wind-sculpted shapes.

Kelp and foam script an alphabet
on blank slate of sand while the bay,
fed by river, nourishes wetlands

behind the dunes. Amorphous drizzle
materializes from nothing. Within our bodies,
organs swell and recede in the rhythm

of salty currents, coming to rest
against a shore of ribcage. Persuaded,
perhaps, by the same celestial power

pulling these tides. Tonight, a harvest
moon will glaze its apple-sweet light
over and into the living waves, fill in

what's left of our footprints. Land ends
where the churning channel begins.
No boat to row, too wild to swim.

IN THE KINGDOM OF ANIMALS

Yosemite National Park, Spring 2020

They emerge from forest brush
and leafy fringe—fox, deer, bobcat, coyote—

jigsaw of creatures hiding in plain sight,
camouflaged within branches

and the red bark of ancient sequoias.
One-by-one, two-by-two as if freed

from the ark, hopscotching from base
of great granite walls to the wet groves

reborn with California poppies.
The black bear wades a glacier-melt stream,

shakes her fur coat, tosses wet rainbows
into air. She lays massive paws

on the warm paved road, listens
to nothingness, licks

meal of anthills with her long pink
tongue; intuits, perhaps, an amen

gratitude beyond her foraging snout—joy
tooth-sharp and tender, reclaiming the kingdom.

BURY THIS

Look how this ordinary creature acrobats
    fence to branch to roof
tightropes eaves   leaps
onto terracotta flower pot
    disturbs begonias and caches
    autumnal bounty, at home
in the city   while
deep in Tillamook Forest
its cousin digs into wilder soil.
    A cedar, celebrated for its enormity,
    salutes coastal sky at the intersection of woodlands
    and highway — surviving disasters of man

and nature and time for 800,
900 years. What is a century
    to this living church?

Salal-fringed path floats above the boggy
    wetlands of Saltair Creek,
a sanctuary where humans
revere ancient growing things—
    jungle-web of limbs
    sprouting fern bouquets
    gnomed and knotty red-barked trunks

new growth atop old growth.

Once, birds dropped random seed here, or
        wind shook loose fertile pods, or
a frenetic squirrel like this one
buried the future where
        a sapling took hold.

THE HERRING GIRLS

Between 1903–1969, young women came from all over Iceland to Siglufjordur,
where they prepared fish for exporting. In 1969, the herring failed to appear,
due to years of overfishing.

We left our fathers' lowland farms—
red-roofed barns, horses grazing the tundra—
for bounty of the north country.
Here, fish undulate in schools so thick
we lean off the boat to touch them.
Herring ripple silver riches by the nautical mile,
pulsing waves of their own making.

We are something now.
Every day we stand on the docks
waiting for boats to arrive—ready
in our oilskin aprons, hands quick and sure
as we hack heads off
the life that had just been swimming,
chuck guts to cats prowling the wharf.

Salted, pickled, smoked, brined—we pack
those fish into coopered barrels by the ton,
our work the pride of a country.

Piers are stacked with crates higher than our reach.
Floes carved by ancient
glaciers drift in the fjord, veined with filaments
of palest blue. All around us: industry's urgent hum,
an abundance hauled into nets for the taking.
Endless hours lit by midnight sun.

The fish, forever running.

IGUANA

Mexico City's gray cinder blocks
     quiver in the haze
as our bus pulls into a wayside

pocked with scrub, brown vegetation,
     arroyo's shallow smear.
Next to the tequila stand, tourists
pay good money to feed a burro bottles
of Coca Cola; for two pesos, snap
a photograph of the woman with an iguana
     atop her head.

That languid creature
flicks a pink tongue, its flagging tail
a tired metronome.
String tied around its neck leashes it close,
a reptilian hat over hot black braided hair.
I argue with my sensibilities for a while,
then toss her a few pesos as the bus drives away.

She's a blur through the window—this woman
whose mother
     gave her a name.
Magenta hummingbirds in flight
across her cotton apron. Baby balanced
on one hip, iguana flopped across her head
as she stoops for those coins,
     little tarnished stars in the dirt.

IN GREECE

after Ursula K. LeGuin

Not long after gulls stopped
wheeling over its wake,
the ferry docked in Kefalonia.
I stood on sun-streaked planks
looking out to the sea that sailed me there.
I came to love the singular color of Ionian blue,
island blue, an impossible blue. Doors
and shutters repeated sky and sea
against white-washed houses on hills.
In the *kafeneon* mustached men
clicked beads of *komboloi*
to pass the time, in every knot
a prayer. Goat bells rang a musical
necklace along the dusty paths.
I don't know if old women still sell gardenias
in kiosks, or if I could find that girl
who wrapped herself in a shawl
of wonder and light.

IF WINGS

So simple. Sometimes you find yourself
emboldened by color, like living in a country
of hothouses—all chartreuse energy, euphoric
mess of Malaysian banana tree leaves, papaya-

syrupy sky sliced with blades of yellow. Here,
orchids and African violets thrive; untethered trumpet
vines slither into a strangled riot of green.
You want to linger, uncertain

how you arrived, so far from salt-
mist fog and cooling canopies. If wings
could carry you up and over a perfumed
red river, would you fly into the heady scent

of gardenias? Wings scissor the silken sky, like gutting
a fish that swallowed a coin. Rainforest's steamy
season vibrates with curious calls of parrots, ripe
with velvet smells. Let yourself taste the life of plants,

the juice of berries shining on their stems.
Wander these gardens guided by
your own compass, a pilgrim in an untamed
found place. Not lost, but turning.

CRIMINAL

Surely the dog was howling when the burglar
climbed through the bathroom window.
Breaking glass in the daylight—even the police
are baffled at what she didn't take: diamond ring,
gold earrings on the dresser, rare books
bound in red leather. Instead, she ate my food
and wore my clothes, slipping into the sleeves of silk
blouses like she was fitting into my life.
In the closet, a winter coat is missing.
I find signs of her in the basin, where she cleaned
herself with jasmine soap that belongs to me.
In the kitchen she chose the ripest fruit,
my favorite cheese to slice. She tried to change
her scent with a new perfume, but I can smell her
on the sheets where she rested for a while.
She captured my parakeet in a cardboard box.
I know she will never return what she took,
and just as if she shattered a hundred vases
I cannot reassemble a sense of calm in this house.
She must have left wearing my slippers.
I can't find them.

KING TIDE

Despite the warnings—or because
of them—we've come to witness
the wilding surf. Spumed crowns
exaggerate their gaudy froth
on what's left of the beach. Stranded
bull kelp bejewels the shore.

We know the cautions, alert
to sneaker waves that want to suck
us into hypothermic void, mudslides,
slick rocks. Logs, already fallen,
already dead, would roll and crush
our bones easily as a bird's ribcage.

We sidle up to danger's edge, its
metallic-salt taste on our tongues.
Voyeurs unfold chairs on the dune
to face the great arena, as if watching
a coronation parade float by.
Sky lowers its clouded bunting as

waves buck out of their chutes,
bellicose and frenzied. We don't know
whether to fear or hallelujah praise them,
and we just can't stop watching.

JANUARY

Gray whales have migrated south,
singing their way into Baja's lagoons.
Calving now, they renew their enormous kind.

It's the season of king tides and a blood moon,
of fleece coats and wool caps.
Trees etch a darker horizon—
bare but for branches clothed in moss,
sentries at the gateway of town.

Windshield wipers syncopate a slower rhythm.
Puddles reflect the sky; the upside
of looking down. The village settles into
the comfort of its own bones,
shaking the final dregs of summer.
Lamps are lit in old cottages along the ridge.
Beach umbrellas hibernate in sheds,
and the bright flame of crocosmia is extinguished.
Locals have returned to the cafe,
knocking wet sand from their boots.
Not much to spend here but time,
those precious coins spilling freely.

Winter sun unlocks a softer light
over scrub of seagrass and low dunes, over
the long sleeve of shore. Three miles to the jetty,
uninterrupted but for creeks ending
their journeys. Dogs run unleashed.
Spray of salt,
frost on sand, prospect of a proper storm.

IN COUNTY CORK

A soft rain greens County Cork, embraces
petals, nourishing boggy knobs.
Hooves clatter above hedges' dark seams
as a grey sky tips its umbrella over pleated
fields into River Ilen. A soft rain
whiskers stone walls, barns, and old cottages,
beads a rosary over the Skibbereen Famine
Graveyard. Boats rise a little higher

in the harbor. Gulls drift air currents like
small kites, drop seed over briny slopes,
crevices and cracks. They take hold, sprout,
swell, regenerate themselves—rooting
fingers under earth along Hunger
Road, nudging the bones of all those nameless.

SEASHELL RESONANCE

Queen conch glides over seabeds in shallow turquoise
waters. She carries a shell-castle on her back—smooth
as a Botticelli cheek, ruffled like peach-colored
petals. Once, my father gifted me that exotic shell
from Jamaica. He brought the sea home
in a suitcase, from a country of hammocks
and tropical waterfalls. When I held it to my ear
I heard waves lapping into a cove.

So many times, I searched low tides along our cold
coast to find those musical pearly shells, until I learned
the facts of science: any cavity held against the ear—
teacup, empty glass—swells a *whoosh whoosh.*
Those creatures live on travel poster cays hot
with white sand—not like this beach

I walk with you now, toward the black-bouldery
jetty. Behind us, the mountain greens
its ancient generations. Our ocean churns January waves,
sand smooth and shining where water touches it
in winter's half-light. We bend to collect washed-in
bounty: clam shells pecked by gulls,
the fragile carapace of a crab, sand dollars we spend together
inside a little rented cottage fueled by the heat of our fire.
Tall trees shadow the room as cedar smoke
dissipates on our skin, clothes, hair.
The fullness of the moment can hold no more.

We stack the cracked and imperfect shells
into a glass jar set on the sill. Uncapped,
a living sound releases itself, faint
and distant and muted. Until we listen, harder.

NEW YEAR, CAPE FALCON

Yesterday's calendar recycled—December's
snowy scene and all the days gone—too late
for wishing them well. Good riddance.
Gone, too, days and nights spun
like taffy into the candy of pure joy.

Today, the world is rinsed clean

as we hike trails curving onto the cape
like a new promise. Highway's hum
surrenders to creek spilling
over bedrock in its final journey: water
to water. Black boulders slick as seals
jut from a puddle the size of small ponds.
The old forest uncorks its soggy carpet,
boots *plop plop* a sucking noise.
Switchbacks tunnel a thicket glistening
with wet salal until the path ends

at Pacific's immensity—without wings
we can go no further, mud-bound in this soup
that is all earth, water, sky. Gulls
plumped up by sea-wind hover above the slope.
Shore pines lean over the abyss, somehow
holding on, for now. We turn away
from that brink, back to the road, walking into
the rest of January.

THE OFFERING

Virtual tour, Japanese Gardens, April 2020

Because the ornamental red gates
of friendship are shut, a drone scripts
visual haiku over gardens we cannot enter.

From above, the deliberate design
reveals itself. Nothing random:
every blossom, every pebble in harmony.
A purpose, even, between
the stones; absence its own metaphor.

Today no one stands on Moon Bridge
to watch the koi flash orange scales,
glittering half-suns.
Cherry trees shed a pink skin onto the garden
of sand raked to ripple dry waves.
The bonsai pavilion opens to sky and distant vistas,
shelters all the little lovelies, alone, clipped
into their coats. No one walks the path
to Heavenly Waterfall or rests on benches
tucked into the mossy hillside.

What is a gift when the offering
cannot be received, incomplete
in its promise?

THE ART OF CAREFUL PRUNING

The leaves have grown too dense, touching
roofs, stealing light from the windows.
The neighbor and I want them tamed,
but not too much. The tree-trimmer nods,
having heard this before. He says he's for hire,
notch by notch. He cinches the buckle on his harness
and shimmies up the tree. Lean and supple
as a birch, he carries an uncommon strength
in his shoulders. He surveys the uncut canvas
of this job, arranging shades of green
with clips from his tool. Every limb he shaves
drops the sky a little closer. From my window, I watch
the neighbor water to the edge of his property,
his spotted dog barking at the base of the tree.
Ours is not a boundary of substance:
what's his is his, and his is there
and mine is here. He glances up as if he hears
me think. What does he see? A woman writing at a table,
crossing tasks off her list. We need these trees,
need the tangle of new growth to obscure the ordinary
even as we cut it back, again and again.

THREE *Last Pour*

IN ATHENS WITH MARGUERITE

As daylight faded and before evening breezes gifted relief, we climbed rickety
stairs to the roof. I could say we were wicks on candles anticipating the match:
spark to flame, the future all around us no matter where we looked. You might
remember it differently—how we rose,

rung by rung, to escape the miserable heat, the weight of air suffocating and still
above dull blocks of buildings, cacophony of taxis and cats that never stopped
howling. Athens without doors: nothing to lock, no reason for a key.

There was a coarse bread with honey, figs, the scent of oregano where steps
cut into the hill. We carried words like bells on our tongues. *Lalouthia:* flowers

hawked from flatbed trucks in the plaza below. Bougainvillea a tangle
of magenta, scarlet, purple spilling from broken pots, poppies sprouting atop
rubble in the alley. Little faces of joy, despite themselves.

Every night widows slow-walked to the domed church on the corner. Veiled
illusions, black as phantoms, they found holy comfort in the sway of incense.
We would never be like them. When finally it was cool and late and dark,

tiny stars winked through the brown haze, tremulous beacons guiding us,
inviting us to come down from the roof, to enter that magnificent city of ruins.

ONE DAY IN JULY

Others before us set bottles along the sill.
We open the cabin door
to step inside a great green shine—
wine bottles lined up like backbones,
spine of the house.
They collect the morning

light then distribute it—kaleidoscope
of blue awash with gold; no corner unlit.
All day we drink
from the borrowed well of that light as if
sourcing never-ending summer. It finds

me reading in a rocking chair, you rinsing
our cups at the sink. Finds us still and in motion
as stars ready themselves for whatever
comes next. How many ways

to see it: nothing lasts.
Not the long arc of this day; not the smell
of grass and smoke caught in your shirt.

Here we are,
bumping into tomorrow—last pour
from the bottle. Enormous view:
swoop of waves, sickle moon unhooking
the soft fabric of sky.

DIGGING FOR FRANCE

In this photo, I am almost six. My father
tells me if I dig deep enough, I will find
France. I shovel and scrape with my hands
while the wet sand collapses in on itself.
As usual, he is distracted, pulling at that pipe
the way he always did, gazing towards the Pacific,
hand angled over his brow as if to salute
some far off place in the distance. Even now,
I wonder what it was he saw.
Behind us sky, seagulls, and sand.
My little gray sturdy brother
busy with his toy cars while I am digging
for France. With my plastic shovel and pail
I scoop my way through the core
of Oregon. I want to be sucked
into the wet hole and pulled out
the other side into a country
of light and long loaves of bread.
It's not here, it's not here, I scream
from that sorry ditch as the muck sticks
to my hair, eyelids and teeth.
My father pulls me onto his lap
and wraps me in a sweater smelling faintly
of him, of stale tobacco and wet collie.
And although he's never been there,
he teaches me words I need to know:
Enfant, rouge, pain au chocolat.

FOOT MASSAGE

My parents never danced in the kitchen—
no flamboyant dip in a red silk
dress, no rakish tilt of the fedora. They swayed
to a predictable rhythm of domesticity:
proper, Presbyterian.
Evenings, with dishes cleared
and children pajamaed, they sat
at opposite ends of the couch.
My mother slipped shoes off,
stretched her legs to nestle
bare feet in my father's lap.
He massaged her left arch and then
the right with strong thumbs,
slowly circling the ankles
to caress her heels. He kneaded crevices
between each toe to touch that tender hollow
on the underside. She settled into cushions,
arranging her feet as a cat would curl,
and like a cat she purred.
Who knew the foot, with all its
tiny bones, could soften and surrender
to pleasure like that. The whole house
mellowed under its lid. Then they rose to
the last choreographed tasks
of the day: latch the doors, dim
the lights—two beats slow, quick
quick slow.

BOOKS FOR THE LIBRARIAN

Before the barcodes and scanners,
before computers and automatic renewals,
she stamped cards tucked into the backs
of borrowed books. Every day she tended
the counter lined with baskets of yellow pencils,
and prowled Dewey-Decimaled stacks
in search of the obscure and forgotten.

She could point out Caracas and Karachi
in an atlas, compute miles to the moon.
What's the main export of Uganda?
A question worth asking, she would say.
What happens to memories the brain sloughs
onto the heap of forgetting, when the weight
of remembering is too much to carry? These days

the library comes to her, rolling in on a cart.
She slips paperback mysteries
under the fold-down seat—sentences a jumble,
plot sliding off the page.
Still, books take her to new places.
She runs her fingers along the spines,
places them face down on her nightstand—
like little tents in a wilderness
she will return to, a story interrupted.

PAINTING AN OLD BARN

East of the Cascades, pass turnoffs to Fossil
and Spray; just before what's left of Unity,
veer left onto a rutted county road.
You won't need a map.
Keep driving as if you could vanish
into the beige sameness of scrub brush
and brown foothills, as if wishing yourself

disappeared into that landscape becoming
Idaho. Where abandoned chicken coops litter
the farmhouse yard, look for a pocked field—
there, set your easel facing the barn.
Paint it rustic. Red, yes, but fading into

its color, the way memories recede.
Simply marry burnt umber with cadmium red
to find the right shade of worn.
Paint it distressed, dilapidated, Rockwell-esque. Find
what you came for: rusted
hinges, heap of reins, wheels stilled by time.

There it is before you, the other side of repair.
Crumbling, bleached, sagging its structure—
ready for the framing. Where are the horses now?

WHEELS

No blue permeates
this edgeless eggshell sky.
From the 10th floor of the care center
we watch fog
dissipate between blocked shapes,
high-rises and new condominiums.
Windows reflect windows, a visual echo.

Wheels of progress, my mother
says of the hammers and hardhats,
orange scaffolding that climbs
higher than trees.
The only wheels here—
her walker with a fold-down seat, adjustable
handlebars she maneuvers
bathroom to bedroom to television,
down the long quiet corridor
with its faint antiseptic smell.

Now I'm the one remembering
the way it used to be. Once,
her window held horizon—
Mount Hood to the east, wearing
its snowy cape, sun rising pinkly
over the mountain.

A tiny balcony opens
to the outside world.
Construction cranes emerge

through mist. We hear
the steady rhythm of buses, cars,
commuters moving between the stoplights,
all those wheels turning, turning
so far below.

MY GRANDMOTHER'S CHINA

My mother gives me her mother's china,
handed down through a chain of daughters
with the story of its luxury.
I hear all over again how my grandmother
mended, made do. Nothing afforded
for the sake of beauty itself but this china,
bought at the Bon Marché with three years of savings.

We box saucers, nest teacups. I have no use
for egg coddlers, soup terrine, fragile cups
with tiny handles. No room in my cupboards.

My extravagance is something different altogether.
Give me a substantial cup, something to wrap
my whole hand around in the morning.
Like this one bought at the Oregon Coast,
where I watched the miracle of whales breaching;
or these, carried home from Oaxaca, Umbria, Santa Fe.
Somewhere in Vermont a mug baked in a kiln
to the color of autumn leaves. When I drink from it,
I smell the earth and the loam and the clay.

"Wedgewood," my mother says, and runs her fingers
around the gold rim. She recalls again her mother's pleasure
at setting these dishes on a crocheted tablecloth,
elegant as an English garden, lively
with red peonies, climbing-rose, and lavender butterflies.

She extends the box to me and I take it.

AN EDUCATION

Marry a doctor, my mother told me
when I was twelve, as she folded towels
and ironed the sheets.
Just as easy to fall in love
with a rich man as a poor man.

She never suggested life
without a husband, that I could find
satisfaction in currency earned
from my own ambition.
Never told me to wander with a map
creased at the contours of curiosity, or
hike to the precipice of awe
overlooking meadows wild
with lupine and bramble rose.
She schooled me in domestic arts,
warned of drudgery—did not
tell me I could bend and sway
without breaking; find comfort
in the house of my own bones.

That I could love a poet.

Now, with all the potatoes peeled
and apples sliced, I sit with my mother,
hunched over the daily crossword.
The accumulations of a long life
arranged around her—crystal goblets
and silver tea set handed down,
for the last time.

Together we ponder seventeen across:
what's an eight-letter word
for an unmarried woman?

LOOSE ENDS

I'm at loose ends, he used to say. Like a puppet, I wondered, arms and legs
dangling, disconnected from its body? Long strings of yarn unspooled from
the skein, a scarf not yet knitted? Perhaps the fray in fabric—the more it's
pulled the more it unravels. Who said it, anyway, ghosting his own un-

finished story? I can't remember if it was the one married to the purity of his
convictions. We slept summer nights in a teepee, rose to mornings soft as
feathers. His thread the green of gentle beginnings, organic smell of grass,
spring's energy. Or, maybe the poet who spun words to sonnets, fluid language

rippling to my core—folded on Japanese paper, origami birds he gave to me.
His thread bohemian black, dark as ancient river stone. My hands would knot these
loose ends, half-scraps and fistful of tangle, but here's gold thread, circling
a bracelet around my wrist, the way our little rented boat circled the bay, loop-

ing netted traps as we hoisted our Dungeness cache to feast on bounty sucked
from claws, wild strawberries, sweet amber wine. A long silken filament coursed
through him as if he had swallowed the sun, lit from within. I pluck at it still.

KIMONO

I remember a blue kimono
dark with flowers, exotic
flowers. Orchids, hibiscus. The kind

that open, lazy and full, to expose
their sticky parts. After bathing
I slipped into its jungle of folds

as you shook perfumed talc.
The fine white dust clung
like pollen to my skin.

I loosened the sash, turning
to face you. My arms jutted
through enormous square sleeves

and I stood like a pale cross backlit
against a wedge of moon.
Something to believe in, you said.

Each time I opened up
that part of me escaped. Small
and flying, beating with furious wings.

GUSTAVO SWIMMING

Gustavo is blind now.
Hearing your voice,
he gropes the side of the bed.
You stroke the long elegant fingers
that once dressed your hair,
then move the length of him
to massage his feet with eucalyptus oil.
You tell him his face
is still pretty, in this way
sparking what spirit remains,
his body denied to you long ago.
Soon you will scatter
his ashes beneath the Golden Gate.
Thirty times you've done this:
watched as chips of bone, gray flecks
that were your friends sink
into the swirling lap of the Pacific.

When Gustavo says he's afraid,
you tell him it's easy, like swimming.
And because you almost died once,
he believes you. Remembers
when he was a child in Panama,
the first time he pushed off
the deep end of the pool,
his father screaming, *kick, kick!*
Remembers diving for coins,
how they flashed like small suns
in their slow descent

to where it was so quiet, an aqua cave
he had climbed into.

You touch a healing balm
to the pulse at his throat,
your fingers cool on his skin.
He feels himself starting to drift,
to glide down through the damp sheets
into the immensity of blue
water surrounding him.
When he opens his eyes, he can see again.

LILACS

Blue latex gloves, surgical mask— the caregiver wheels our mother, *tick tick* down the linoleum floor to a room with windows latched. Outside, the attendant arranges chairs for our appointment. The distance between us

a pane of glass. Her hands shake a little as we dial into sterile numbness of shelter for the usual conversation: children, grandchildren, great-grand-children; the weather, which today is painting Monet pastels. Lilacs blousy

in the breeze like lacy petticoats. Bees dive into a soft purple underbelly with euphoric dizziness, drunk on their lavender fervor. It's better, we tell ourselves, that she will soon forget we came, carrying as we do this weariness of fear,

illness, politics. Didn't she already endure the Great Depression? Oh, she remembers those days and her one-school town. Hand-me-down coats, years with no Christmas candy. The map in her brain can still trace blue veins of

streets to the Presbyterian church where she sang the psalms of survival. Through our shared window she points to gnarled and knuckled branches of lilac trees on the grounds, waves to them as if greeting an old friend.

Wonders whether they have returned this year in their April gloriousness
 to the graveyard next to the church.

FADE

Prayer flags strung across the lattice
invite you to enter all

earthly dimensions: north, south, east, west,
and center. Center, its own direction—

sucking you into the vortex, until you see again
your mother pinning cotton sheets to a clothesline.

They hover side-by-side
like a flock of angels, billowing

celestial gowns as a breeze shakes
dampness away. Colors

dimmed and softened, the way seasons
meld into themselves—orange becoming apricot, yellows

like melted butter. They wrap you into a sleep
striped with mauve and rose of Sharon, holding

the smell of sun-rinsed summer
you want to bottle.

But it all fades—scent, fabric, memories bleeding
into a watercolor wash, just as these

little square cloths are meant to ravel and fray,
purer in fragility. Creased in shadow, folded in light—

waving tattered hems hello or goodbye:
it doesn't matter which.

FOUND ART

I rummage through her kitchen drawers
and cupboards; peer behind rows of empty
mason jars and mismatched cups to find
some semblance of the person who lived here.
This is no estate. Just another run-down vacated house
with a price affixed to bric-a-brac and Naugahyde chairs.
How much for these Austrian figurines?
Even her hospital bed knocked down in cost.

Broken rakes and a rusted mower guard
remains of the decayed garden and there,
among half-emptied potting soil bags, I spot
driftwood tossed aside with other remnants
of her life no one wants. She painted those pieces
in a vibrant palette: hued in purple, blue, pink.
Mystical creatures emerge from the wood, born
from her dreams—smiling reptile, seahorse,
lavender whale. She prowled water's edge

after storms, bent at the mouth of the huge unknown,
poking through flotsam come to rest along the shore.
Measured with eyes and hands bounty washed in,
and blessed those limbs that had lived in a forest,
miles and rivers and years away.

This one I take—woman with flowing turquoise hair,
arms raised in a sway
shaped by curves in the wood, a joyful dance.
It must have been her, once.

KODACHROME

Limp and unsnappable, these rubber bands
no longer bundle letters
and photographs scattered on the vacant
bedroom floor.
Snapshots pried from frames,
overstuffing shoeboxes—Rome over there,

next to the pile of Paris. Here she is,
serenaded by a gondolier. Eating tapas in Barcelona.
Or was it Madrid? Seville?

Our mother never emptied a single
cupboard or drawer. The faux fireplace
with its switch-on flame
won't burn these photos. Too many for her
one room at the care center; we don't know
which she wants, what she remembers.

Heavy-duty plastic bags destined
for landfill's graveyard overwhelm the dumpster
with faded images of eternal cities
with bridges—always a river, always a bridge.

Our mother's face, young
and smiling, as she enters some great and beautiful
cathedral, posing from the other side of the camera
with a look that says: *I am here.*

WINGS

We sipped Turkish coffee in the plaka,
swirling coarse grounds
that stained our porcelain cups.

I don't remember what destiny was left
in those dregs. I only remember

      August heat as its own ponderous presence,
large and looming, hovering
a white haze over Athens.

It was then, our bones slow and heavy,
we rented a room bare in necessity:
      bed, window, half-enchanted view.

Heat coursed through him like a juice
squeezed from the sun, seeping
between hollows and curves,
through sweet mounds of flesh
down to his tanned feet.
      It was not love

that took us there; rather, a coolness
bought by the hour. A ceiling fan ticked
      its metal wings, whirred occasional relief.

We waited until the sun quit the sky
so the moon could rise over ruins;
until a restless flutter of breeze
caused the curtains to sway and gray cats
in the alley howled again.

PARIAH

William Charles Roach, died by suicide January 6, 1916

William, I have searched for you
in cemetery logs and through dusty
obituaries written a century ago.
That's the problem with being dead
so long. You're nothing more than a footnote
on the family tree, black rag of mourning.
I'm just saying, sooner
or later every story reveals another truth.
Even after three generations gone,
I want to know yours.

As suicides go, yours was spectacular,
carried out with aplomb. No if-I-should-die-
before-I-wake sleeping pill.
No quiet hanging from an attic
rafter. You could have walked, pocket full
of stones, into the oil-slicked channel.

No, your death the opposite of drowning,
in a fury of flames. Forever the pariah.
You abandoned wife and daughters
to hardscrabble life, and worse:
a future of unforgiven bitterness.

No one remembers you now, or that pain
so potent you exorcized it by fire.
No one is left living to tell me
whether you wanted to die, or if
you were reaching for the hand of mercy.

FRANKIE

I might have known he would refuse
the sunken cheek of a burial plot,
graveyard irrigated with cemetery hoses.

He was a bottle that couldn't be stoppered;
his passport stamped with the countries
      of tango, bossa nova and samba.

Now handfuls of Frankie green the hills above
Portland, and he drifted a while from a bridge
over the Willamette. I smuggled a baggie
into the stadium, where he liked to watch boys
take practice swings. He floated all over the infield
and when the pitcher squeezed the rosin bag:
      poof.

His ashes mix with Mexican sand; he's in Barcelona,
on Castro Street, settled into the silt of a coastal stream.
And, let's just say Francois dusts
a few geraniums along the Champs Élysées.

Now I stand with a decorative urn in the rose garden
overlooking a silhouetted city. He would tell me
to leave him in the backside of a shadow, to look
for him in negative space,
where he reverberates with the energy of jazz
      blue dynamic
      between the notes.

There's still so much of him left.

IMMIGRATION STORY

Volcanic ash grayed the air when hens refused
to lay, confusing day from night.
Ice floes choked harbors, freezing over the fish.
Blizzards, sheep disease, famine and smallpox.

Margaret, at 12—half-woman, half-child—stood on the deck
as she sailed from Akureyri, watching her homeland
disappear. That place of biting beauty
     she would never know again.
Goodbye to the small country of farms
defined by its seasons:
     cold, frozen, snowmelt and mud.

The ship bullied its way through headwinds and seasickness,
docking at last in Canada.
Papers and documents, immigration sheds in Toronto.
The strange clattering sound of steel rails.
     No trains in Iceland.

They hacked at wilderness for others' profit—
felling trees, grubbing stumps, blasting granite.
More men than jobs, more hunger than food.
So many babies died in the shanties; buried in tiny unmarked
graves next to the Burnt River.

Here's a photograph of Margaret at 20, married
in the Dakota Territory. Her face round and doughy, eyes
the palest color of Icelandic pools. See how
her twelve children branch the family tree.

Here are our passports; a map of roads ringing
the island. We drive past fjords and glaciers, past
tidy villages with red-steepled churches—
all the way to the north-country farmland she left.
We have come this far to see for the first time
what she saw for the last. Here, we find our names.

ACKNOWLEDGMENTS

I am grateful to the editors of the following journals and other publications where these poems first appeared, sometimes in earlier versions:

The Adirondack Review: "Amanda's Trail"

Calyx: "Gustavo Swimming," "Letter to the Disappeared" (finalist for 2020 Lois Cranston Memorial Poetry Prize)

Catamaran Literary Reader: "Found Art"

Cathexis Northwest: "Books for the Librarian," "In the Commonwealth"

Cirque: "Terminus"

The Ekphrastic Review: "American Loggers, 1939"

Gyroscope Review: "Wings"

Hoffman Center for the Arts: "Digging for France" (winner of 2020 Neahkahnie Mountain Poetry Prize), "Lilacs," "If Wings," "In Greece"

North Coast Squid: "January," "Frankie"

Oregon Poetry Association Pandemic Anthology: "In the Kingdom of Animals," "Neither/Nor"

Rain Magazine: "Pariah"

VerseWeavers: "In Athens with Marguerite"

VoiceCatcher: "Iguana," "My Grandmother's China"

Whistling Willow: Tree Poems: "Tree"

Willamette Week: "Kimono," "Criminal"

Willawaw Journal: "Foot Massage"

Windfall: "New Year, Cape Falcon," "The Offering"

This book is many years—decades, in fact—in the making. I am grateful to my fellow poet-editors at Airlie Press—Brittney Corrigan, Amelia Díaz Ettinger, Jennifer Perrine and Jennifer Reimer—for helping me realize this dream, and for steering the manuscript throughout its iterations. Over the years, I have had the opportunity to study with many amazing poets and teachers, including Kim Addonizio, John Brehm, Kim Stafford, Emily Ransdell, and Joseph Millar. They have all contributed in significant ways to my development as a poet. Special gratitude to Jannie Dresser, who launched me on this journey with a workshop in her Berkeley apartment, and to John Sibley Williams, an excellent teacher who provided extraordinary critique, guidance, and support throughout the development of this collection.

Airlie Press is grateful to the following sponsors and individuals,
whose contributions provided major support in funding this
and other Airlie Press books of poetry.

Joelle Barrios

Joanie Campf

Jane Comerford

Chip Ettinger

Cecilia Hagan

Quinton Hallett

Dennis Harper

Donna Henderson

Hannah Larabee

John Laurence

Karen McPherson

Alida Rol

Kat Sanchez

Literary Arts
FIND YOUR STORY HERE

OREGON ARTS
COMMISSION

Oregon
Community
Foundation

Regional Arts &
Culture Council

Beaverton
OREGON

ABOUT THE PUBLISHER

Airlie Press is run by writers. A nonprofit publishing collective, the press is dedicated to producing beautiful and compelling books of poetry. Its mission is to offer a shared-work publishing alternative for writers working in the Pacific Northwest. Airlie Press is supported by book sales, grants, and donations. All funds return to the press for the creation of new books of poetry.

COLOPHON

The book type is set in Arno, a typeface inspired early humanist typefaces of the 15th and 16th centuries. Letterforms were cast in metal to imitate hand-written minuscule and printed, these innovations by Aldus Manutius also brought the invention of the italic in 1501. Released by Adobe in 2007, Arno was designed by Robert Slimbach to have contemporary appearance and function: the optically-sized fonts represent the scale of the pen to its corresponding point size, and each features expressive italic swash sets.

Printed in Portland, Oregon, USA